United States Presidents

Andrew Jackson

Series Consultant:
Don M. Coerver, professor of history
Texas Christian University, Fort Worth, Texas

Karen Judson

Enslow Publishers, Inc.

40 Industrial Road   PO Box 38
Box 398   Aldershot
Berkeley Heights, NJ 07922   Hants GU12 6BP
USA   UK

http://www.enslow.com

Library of Congress Cataloging-in-Publication Data

Judson, Karen, 1941–
    Andrew Jackson / Karen Judson.
       p. cm. — (United States presidents)
    Includes bibliographical references and index.
    Summary: A biography of the seventh president from his childhood in South
    Carolina, through his military career in the War of 1812, to his legacy as
    America's first populist president.
      ISBN 0-89490-831-6
      1. Jackson, Andrew, 1767–1845—Juvenile literature. 2. Presidents—United
    States—Biography—Juvenile literature. [1. Jackson, Andrew, 1767–1845.
    2. Presidents.] I. Title. II. Series.
    E382.J87   1997
    973.5'6'092—dc21

    [B]   97-9051
                                                  CIP
                                                      AC

Printed in the United States of America

10 9 8 7 6 5 4 3

To Our Readers: All Internet Addresses in this book were active and appropriate at
the time we went to press. Any comments or suggestions can be sent by e-mail to
Comments@enslow.com or to the address on the back cover.

Contents

Acknowledgment

The author wishes to thank William H. Davis of the Archival Programs Branch, Center for Legislative Archives, National Archives, Washington, D.C., for his generous assistance in locating and photocopying documents written during President Jackson's two terms in office.

1

THE PEOPLE'S CHOICE

A lthough he had just been elected President of the United States, Andrew Jackson had mixed emotions. "I am filled with gratitude," he wrote to his best friend, John Coffee, after learning the results of the November 1828 election. "Still, my mind is depressed."[1]

Jackson was tired after a long and brutal campaign. His political rivals had been especially cruel toward Mrs. Jackson. They made fun of her "dowdyfied figure" (Mrs. Jackson was plump), and her "inelegant conversation." They said she had a "total want of refinement," because she smoked a pipe and also enjoyed cigars.[2] Also, vicious rumors were spread about the Jacksons' marriage.

When Jackson was elected President in 1828, he

and his wife Rachel had been happily married for nearly thirty-eight years. The courtship between Andrew Jackson and Rachel Donelson Robards began in 1788. Rachel was living with her widowed mother at the time. Jackson, a young single attorney, rented a room at Mrs. Donelson's boardinghouse in Nashville, Tennessee.

Rachel Donelson had married Captain Lewis Robards when she was seventeen, but the marriage was troubled from the beginning. Robards was wildly jealous of his beautiful, spirited, young wife and he did not treat her well. He decided that a young lawyer named Peyton Short, who boarded in the Robards home in Kentucky, was paying too much attention to Rachel. He sent his wife to live with her mother. Although Robards later begged Rachel to come home, the marriage was beyond repair.

Rachel Robards and Andrew Jackson were both twenty-four years old when they met. They liked many of the same things and were attracted to each other from the start. Shortly after Rachel met Andrew Jackson, her estranged husband, Lewis Robards, filed for divorce. When she married Jackson in August of 1791, both she and Andrew believed her divorce from Robards was final.

In December of 1793, Jackson chanced upon court records stating that Lewis Robards had recently been granted a divorce, on grounds that Rachel Robards had left her husband and was living with another man. Jackson discovered that the marriage between Rachel

Hannah was the household slave who cared for Rachel Jackson.

and Lewis Robards had not been legally over until September 27, 1793.

Robards had led Rachel to believe that a divorce had been granted in 1791, although he had not published notice in an area newspaper for eight weeks, as was required by law. In fact, Robards had waited two years to sue for divorce, perhaps to spite Rachel. On January 17, 1794, Andrew and Rachel Jackson were married for the second time.

As the presidential campaign of 1828 heated up, Jackson's political foes spread the story of the two weddings. Rachel was called a bigamist (someone who is illegally married to two persons at the same time). Jackson was labeled a wife stealer and a liar.

Rachel was a friendly, kind, and religious woman. During the campaign, she showed little emotion over the shameful stories that were told. However, she was apparently not eager to become First Lady, because after the election she remarked, "For Mr. Jackson's sake I am glad. For my own part I never wished it."[3]

A friend who visited Rachel Jackson at her home after the election reported a shocking change in her: "From that moment her energy subsided, her spirits drooped, and her health declined. She has been heard to speak but seldom since."[4]

Rachel Jackson's health failed. She developed a cough and had trouble breathing. On December 17, 1828, Mrs. Jackson complained of a piercing pain in her side. A doctor was called, but Rachel had suffered what was probably a major heart attack and there was little that could be done for her.

Jackson stayed by his wife's bedside for the next few days. She seemed to grow stronger. Then on December 22, Rachel suddenly cried out, "I am fainting," and collapsed into the arms of her maid, Hannah.[5] Mrs. Jackson died during the night. Jackson sat by his wife's side for hours, hoping that she might wake up. He refused all food and drink. Finally, Jackson had to accept that Rachel was gone. On December 24, Rachel Jackson was buried in the garden of the Hermitage.

The Hermitage, the Tennessee home of Andrew and Rachel Jackson, as it appears today.

(The Hermitage was the name given to the Jackson home near Nashville, Tennessee.) When she died, Mrs. Jackson was sixty-one years old.

Jackson visited Rachel's grave a few days after her funeral. As he stood with family members, he cried, "She was murdered—murdered by slanders that pierced her heart! May God Almighty forgive her murderers as I know she forgave them. I never can!"[6]

After Rachel Jackson's funeral, Andrew Jackson was not well and was clearly suffering over his wife's death. People wondered if the newly elected President could make the trip to Washington. If he took the oath of office, would he be able to stand the pressures of the presidency?

The President-elect and his party left Tennessee by steamboat on January 19, 1829. They arrived in Washington, D.C., three weeks later, on February 11. Among those traveling with Jackson were his twenty-year-old adopted son, Andrew Jackson, Jr.; his nephew, Andrew Donelson; and Donelson's wife, Emily. Donelson was to be President Jackson's private secretary, and Emily would act as hostess in the White House. Jackson's son would return to the Hermitage as caretaker after the inauguration.

The Jackson party quietly arrived in Washington. When President Jackson finally was seen in public, he was dressed all in black. He also wore a black armband and a black band around his tall beaver hat.

Although Jackson still mourned his wife's death, he

Andrew Jackson, Jr., the adopted son of President and Mrs. Jackson, accompanied his father on his trip to his inauguration at Washington, D.C.

forced himself to focus on his new job as chief executive of the United States. He spent the next few weeks choosing members of his cabinet and writing his inaugural address. In his speech, he thanked the people for "the honor conferred" on him. He admitted his "solemn apprehensions for the safety of the great and important interests committed to my charge."[7]

To show his appreciation to all those who had supported him in his run for President, Jackson invited everyone to come to Washington for his inauguration. Afterward, guests were also invited to a levee (reception) in the White House.

Wednesday, March 4, 1829, the day of President Jackson's inauguration, dawned clear and sunny in Washington, D.C. For the first time, the swearing-in ceremony would be held outdoors, on the east portico (porch) of the Capitol. An outdoor ceremony had been planned to make room for all the people who had come to watch General Andrew Jackson take the oath of office.

At 11:00 A.M., Jackson, dressed in mourning black, left the hotel where he was staying. He marched down Pennsylvania Avenue with soldiers from the Revolutionary War and the War of 1812 at his side. Jackson was six feet tall and weighed one hundred and forty pounds. At age sixty-one, his thick reddish hair had turned white. As he marched with his fellow soldiers, observers said that the solemn Jackson looked more "presidential" than any President since George Washington.

SOURCE DOCUMENT

City of Washington
March 2d 1829.

Sir,

Thro you I beg leave to inform the Senate, that on Wednesday, the 4th instant at 12 oclock, I shall be ready to take the oath prescribed by the constitution, previously to entering on a discharge of my official duties, and at such place as the Senate may think proper to designate.

I am, very respectfully,
Sir, your Ob.t Serv.t

Andrew Jackson

J. C. Colhoun
vice President of
the United States.

This letter from Andrew Jackson to the Senate informed members that he would be ready to take the oath of office on Wednesday, March 4, 1829.

When he reached the Capitol, Jackson watched the swearing-in of Vice President John C. Calhoun in the Senate chamber. After the Vice President had taken his oath of office, the President went to the east portico of the Capitol Building. Twenty thousand people cheered as General Jackson bowed to the "majesty of the people."[8]

Jackson gave his inaugural speech, then took the oath of office. (Today the President takes the oath first, then speaks.) President Jackson's inaugural address was one of the shortest in history, lasting just ten minutes. After Jackson's speech, Chief Justice of the Supreme Court John Marshall gave him the oath of office.

Later, Jackson's friend, a Kentucky newspaper reporter Amos Kendall, wrote about the mood of the crowd. "It was a proud day for the people," he said. "General Jackson is their own president."[9]

General Jackson was called the "People's Choice." However, there were those who did not like him and thought he should not have been elected. Some believed he was too hot-tempered, too set in his ways, too common, and too uneducated to be President. Joseph Story, an associate justice of the Supreme Court, spoke for this group when he described the noisy crowd of Jackson supporters on the day of the inauguration. "The reign of King 'Mob' seemed triumphant," he said.[10]

As soon as President Jackson finished his speech, the excited crowd broke through chain barriers and rushed

---

SOURCE DOCUMENT

As long as our Government is administered for the good of the people, and is regulated by their will; as long as it secures to us the rights of person and of property, liberty of conscience and of the press, it will be worth defending. . . .

(First Inaugural Address, March 4, 1829)

In his brief inaugural address, Andrew Jackson discussed the government as the protector of American liberties.

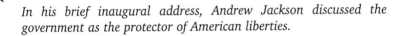

toward him. United States marshals freed Jackson from the mob. They led the President out of the west entrance of the Capitol Building, where a horse was waiting to take him back to the White House.

When Jackson arrived at the White House, it was full of people. Some had come as far as five hundred miles for the occasion—on horseback, in wagons, and on foot. Trays of food and barrels of punch had been prepared by White House servants. Before waiters could serve the rowdy mob, they pushed forward and grabbed the food and drink. Punch splashed over the floor; food was ground into the carpets. Men in muddy boots climbed onto satin-covered chairs to glimpse the President. Furniture was smashed and several thousand dollars worth of glassware and china was broken by the crowd.

The crush of people eager to shake hands with the President nearly smothered Jackson. To keep the

President safe, his friends sneaked him out the back door of the White House.

At 4:00 P.M., Jackson went back to his hotel, where he spent his first night as President of the United States. Since he was mourning the death of his wife, President Jackson did not attend the inaugural ball held that night in his honor.

Later, there were many different opinions about the inaugural celebration. Some onlookers called the behavior of the crowd shocking. Others called the inauguration a huge success. "It was a proud day for the people," said the newspaper, *Argus of Western America,* on March 18, 1829.

> General Jackson is their own President. Plain in his dress, venerable in his appearance, unaffected and familiar in his manners, he was greeted by them with an enthusiasm which bespoke him the Hero of a popular triumph.[11]

Settlers, frontiersmen, and soldiers liked General Jackson. In fact, he had been fondly nicknamed "Old Hickory" by the troops he commanded during the War of 1812 against Great Britain. However, there were others who saw Jackson as violent, hot-tempered, and ill-mannered. These Americans questioned what kind of President he would make.

However history would judge the occasion, Andrew Jackson's inauguration marked a first in America. The six Presidents who had come before him had served the country well. However, former Presidents had been chosen more by Congress and others with power than

Andrew Jackson, who was in mourning at the time of his inauguration as President, kept this portrait of his late wife, Rachel, beside his bed.

by the people. With Jackson, for the first time, the people themselves had chosen the President. The citizens voted into office the man they most wanted to see in the White House. The voters knew that Old Hickory would not be afraid of Congress and would defend their liberty to the best of his ability.

2

A FRONTIER BEGINNING

L ike many American settlers of his day, Andrew Jackson was born to poor immigrant parents. His family had sailed from Larne, Ireland, in April 1765. Jackson's parents, Andrew Jackson, Sr., and Elizabeth Hutchinson Jackson, had to leave Ireland when their farm failed. They brought their two small sons—two-year-old Hugh and five-month-old Robert— to America to begin a new life. (Andrew Jackson, Jr., had not yet been born.)

After a hard voyage by ship across the Atlantic Ocean, the Jackson family landed near Philadelphia, Pennsylvania, in May 1765. Shortly after their arrival in America, Andrew Jackson, Sr., his wife, and their two sons joined other immigrants headed for the Carolina frontier, five hundred miles overland.

Elizabeth Jackson's four sisters and their husbands had already settled in an area called the Waxhaws, or the Waxhaw Settlement, near the border of North and South Carolina. The settlement had been named "Waxhaw" after a Native American tribe that had once lived in the region.

After just five years in America, Elizabeth's older sister, Jane, and her husband, James Crawford, were wealthy Waxhaw landowners. Andrew Jackson, Sr., and Elizabeth hoped to do as well. They bought a small piece of land near the Crawfords, built a cabin, and began clearing their land to farm.

Two days before Elizabeth Jackson was to give birth to their third son, her husband was hurt while trying to move a large log. Frontier medical care was limited to home remedies, and Andrew, Sr., was too badly injured to be helped. He died three days later. The new baby was born March 15, 1767, at the home of the Crawfords in South Carolina. He was named Andrew, after his father.

With her husband gone, Elizabeth Jackson was left alone to care for her three sons. Since she had no way to support her family, the Jacksons moved in with Jane and James Crawford. Jane had been ill for several years and soon died. After Jane's death, Elizabeth did spinning and weaving and looked after the eleven children in the household, including the eight Crawford youngsters and the three Jackson brothers.

As a child, Andrew Jackson was a quick learner. He

could read by the age of five, and at nine he became a "public reader." Since many of the settlers could not read, public readers were chosen to read aloud from newspapers. The story is told, but has never been confirmed, that Andrew Jackson read the Declaration of Independence to his neighbors when it was published in newspapers during the summer of 1776.

Long before the Declaration of Independence was written, trouble was brewing between the American colonists and their English rulers. The colonists resented the high taxes imposed by Great Britain, and the searches of their homes and businesses by British soldiers who were looking for taxable items. There were frequent clashes between colonists in New York and Massachusetts and the British soldiers stationed in New England.

By 1773, most taxes on imports to the American colonies had been repealed by the British government. However, the tax on tea was left in place, as a display of power by Great Britain. When three British ships loaded with tea sailed into Boston Harbor, local citizens would not permit the cargo to be unloaded. The royal governor of Massachusetts, Thomas Hutchinson, would not let the ships return to England until the tax was paid. On the night of December 16, 1773, a group of Boston citizens, led by Samuel Adams, boarded the ships. The men, some of whom were dressed as Native Americans, threw crates of tea from the ship's hold into the water, then escaped. Colonists cheered when news of the "Boston Tea Party" reached them.

England's King George III closed Boston Harbor. Farmers in the Waxhaws quickly joined other colonists in sending food and supplies to the landlocked Bostonians.

In March 1774, the British Parliament passed four laws, called the Coercive Acts, to punish the colony of Massachusetts. The Boston Port Act closed the port of Boston until local citizens paid the East India Company for the ruined tea. The Massachusetts Government Act canceled the colony's charter and limited town meetings to one a year. The Quartering Act called for colonists to provide places for British soldiers to stay. The

Andrew Jackson and his family in South Carolina were among those who cheered the Boston Tea Party as a step toward American independence from Great Britain.

Administration of Justice Act said British officials would be tried in England, instead of Massachusetts courts, when accused of certain crimes. Colonists called the laws Intolerable Acts. The acts led to the meeting of the First Continental Congress in 1774.

In September and October of 1774, delegates from the First Continental Congress met in Philadelphia, Pennsylvania. Parliament and the king refused to change British policy and war seemed certain. "The die is now cast," said England's King George III. "The colonies must either submit or triumph."[1]

A few American colonists, called Tories or Loyalists, remained loyal to Great Britain. Most of the colonists, however, were in favor of American independence. This group called themselves the Patriots or Whigs.

A group of Patriots near Boston boasted that they could be ready for battle at a minute's notice. The British heard that these "minutemen" stored their weapons in Concord, Massachusetts, twenty miles from Boston. On April 18, 1775, British troops marched toward Concord and Lexington, planning to take the weapons. Two Patriots, Paul Revere and William Dawes, volunteered to ride to Concord to warn the minutemen. Revere and Dawes made their famous midnight ride, and as a result, the minutemen were waiting for the British when they reached Concord. The Patriots drove the British redcoats back to Boston.

Six thousand American troops surrounded Boston,

preventing the British troops from leaving. The American Revolution had begun.

Many Waxhaw men soon volunteered to fight the British. In June of 1776, Andrew Jackson's uncle, Robert Crawford, led troops made up of men and boys from the Waxhaws to Charleston, South Carolina, to prevent British ships from landing in the harbor. Their mission was successful and the militia returned to Waxhaw.

War raged in the Northeast over the next three years, but it did not reach the Waxhaws. Life was hard for Elizabeth Jackson and her three sons during this time, but her hopes for the future rested in her youngest son, Andrew. Perhaps the restless Andrew would not go to war, his mother reasoned, if she could persuade him to go to school to become a preacher.

However, young Andrew was not interested in school and skipped classes whenever he could. In 1778, at the age of eleven, he joined a cattle drive to Charleston, South Carolina. Afterward, with the money earned from the sale of her portion of the herd, Mrs. Jackson sent Andrew to a school near their home, where Mr. William Humphries, the local teacher, taught him to read and write. The school closed in 1780 and it was some time before Jackson entered a classroom again.

At age thirteen, Andrew Jackson's favorite activities were running, jumping, wrestling, shooting, and racing horses. He was quick to fight if he thought others were making fun of him and he became known for his hot temper. One Waxhaw boy later recalled Jackson as "the only bully he had ever known who was not also a coward."[2]

As Andrew Jackson was growing into the tall, lanky man he would become, Waxhaw settlers watched the fighting in the Northeast. Then in 1779, the British marched through Georgia and into South Carolina. Robert Crawford's Waxhaw militia was again called to fight. This time Andrew's oldest brother, Hugh Jackson, joined them.

At a place called Stono Ferry in South Carolina, Crawford's volunteers drove the British back into Georgia. Hugh Jackson fell ill before the battle but did not obey orders not to fight. He collapsed when the fighting was over and died a short time later.

In 1780, the British landed in Charleston. They captured Robert Crawford but released him when he promised not to fight again. Crawford went home and quickly reorganized his militia.

The British continued their push through the South. Elizabeth, Andrew, and Robert Jackson fled with other Waxhaw settlers to safety in North Carolina. When they went home a few weeks later, Andrew, thirteen, and Robert, sixteen, joined the South Carolina militia.

In April 1781, Andrew and Robert Jackson had just returned to Waxhaw from another flight to safety in North Carolina, this time for three months. They approached a house near Waxhaw, not knowing British soldiers were inside, and were captured.

After the two boys were captured, a British officer ordered Andrew Jackson to clean his boots. Jackson refused, stating that he was a prisoner of war, not a servant. The angry officer drew his sword and raised it to strike. Jackson threw up his left arm to ward off the blow. The officer slashed at him, cutting the boy's fingers to the bone. The blow also opened a deep gash on Jackson's head. When Robert Jackson also refused to clean the officer's boots, his head, too, was gashed by the soldier's sword.

Denied medical treatment and bleeding from their wounds, the two Jackson brothers were marched to prison in Camden, forty miles away. There, Andrew and

The Revolutionary War came close to Andrew Jackson's South Carolina home when the British attacked American troops at the Battle of Camden in May 1780.

Robert were lucky to be fed stale bread and water once a day. Too weak to defend himself, Andrew's coat and shoes were stolen. The two brothers also caught small-pox. Elizabeth Jackson rode to Camden and persuaded the stockade's commanding officer to release her sons and three other Waxhaw boys. Although they were finally free, Robert was near death and Andrew was very ill.

On the trip home, Robert was strapped to a horse while Andrew walked beside him. Although Robert survived the journey, he died two days later. Andrew spent weeks in bed, near death, but finally recovered his health. Later, he described his bout with smallpox. "When it left me I was a skeleton—not quite six feet long and a little over six inches thick! It took me all the rest of that year to recover my strength and get flesh enough to hide my bones."[3]

When Andrew had finally recovered, Elizabeth Jackson left him and went with two other women to Charleston, South Carolina. The women served as nurses for sick American prisoners on British prison ships. Mrs. Jackson was especially concerned about two of her nephews, who had been captured by the British. Along with many other prisoners, her nephews were suffering from cholera, also known as "ship fever." As Elizabeth said good-bye to her son, she gave him this advice: "Make friends by being honest, keep them by being steadfast."[4]

"Andy . . . never tell a lie, nor take what is not your

own, nor sue . . . for slander . . .," she added. "Settle them cases yourself."[5]

Andrew Jackson never saw his mother again. She died of cholera in the fall of 1781 and was buried in an unmarked grave near Charleston. At fourteen, Andrew was an orphan. "I felt utterly alone," he said, "and tried to recall her last words to me."[6]

3

FROM DRIFTER TO GENTLEMAN

After his mother died, Andrew Jackson went to live with his uncle, Thomas Crawford. He did not get along with his uncle and left after a short time. Jackson then went to live with Joseph White, another relative, to learn saddle making. He left White's home after just six months.

After he left his relatives, Jackson could not decide what to do with his life. He ran with a band of wild young men who spent most of their time playing cards and betting on horse races and cockfights. (Cockfighting still exists in some places. It is a cruel sport where roosters fight to the death, while bettors wager which animal will kill the other first.) Since his relatives did not approve of his behavior, Jackson seldom saw them.

In 1782, while Jackson was trying to decide what to do with his life, the defeated British army left Charleston. (The American Revolution ended at Yorktown, Virginia, on October 19, 1781. On that date, British General Charles Cornwallis surrendered to General George Washington, commander of the American Continental Army.) About this time, Jackson received word from an attorney in Charleston that his grandfather had died in Ireland, leaving him three hundred pounds. In 1782, this was about one thousand dollars in United States currency—a fortune to the fifteen-year-old Andrew. Jackson left Waxhaw for Charleston at once, to claim his inheritance.

In Charleston, Jackson moved into the Quarter Horse Tavern, an expensive hotel. He bought several new suits of clothes for himself, then made friends with a group of young men. Since he and his new friends spent most of their time betting on horses at the local race track, Jackson's money did not last long. Soon his hotel bill was three weeks overdue and he could not pay it.

Then Jackson walked past a group of men throwing dice. The gamblers admired his horse and invited him to join the game. Jackson bet his horse, hoping to win enough money to pay his bills. He decided if he lost his horse he would give his landlord his saddle and bridle, as partial payment of his bill, then walk back to Waxhaw. He threw the dice and won two hundred dollars. ". . . Being successful, I had new spirits infused into me," Jackson said.[1]

Jackson left Charleston, determined to do something worthwhile with his life. Years later he claimed that when he walked away a winner in Charleston, he never again played dice.

From Charleston, Jackson rode back to the Waxhaws. He attended school for one year in Charlotte, North Carolina. He may have taught school in Waxhaw for one year. In December 1784, a few weeks before his eighteenth birthday, Jackson left the Waxhaws forever. He had heard that lawyers were needed on the frontier. He rode to Salisbury, North Carolina, about seventy-five miles away, to begin studying law.

Spruce Macay, an attorney in Salisbury, trained young men in the law. Macay accepted Jackson as a student. In Jackson's day, one did not have to attend college or law school to become a lawyer. Students worked with a licensed attorney for a year or two, then took an exam given by a judge. If they passed the exam, they were licensed to practice law.

In Salisbury, Jackson studied the law, but he also enjoyed local society. The young ladies found him attractive, but a bit wild. Everyone who met him noticed his steely blue eyes. "Jackson had now reached the full height of manhood, cadaverously lean, though strong, wiry, and supple, with an air of almost compulsive eagerness in his bearing . . .," wrote Burke Davis. "His pale, pocked face was arresting if not handsome, and his forehead was marked with a scar that ran into his mop of auburn hair . . ."[2]

Jackson worked for Macay until 1786, then left to work with another North Carolina lawyer, Colonel John Stokes. Stokes had lost a hand fighting in the American Revolution and in its place he wore a silver knob. He liked to make a point or call for attention in court by banging the knob loudly on a table.

After studying with Stokes for six months, Jackson passed his exam. He received his license to practice law on September 26, 1787.

Jackson began practicing law, but still could not decide where he wanted to settle. Then he heard that John McNairy, a friend and fellow student at Spruce Macay's, had been elected superior court judge for the Western District of North Carolina. McNairy had to choose a public prosecutor for the district and he promised the job to Jackson.

In the spring of 1788, soon after he was named public prosecutor, Jackson, along with McNairy and three or four other officers of the court, headed for a wilderness area in what is now eastern Tennessee. They planned to go first to the town of Jonesborough. From there they would push westward through two hundred miles of wilderness, to Nashville in the Cumberland River Valley.

Jackson's party reached Jonesborough in May 1788. Travel in small groups was dangerous, so they decided to stay put until they could join a larger party traveling west. During the four months they waited in

Jonesborough, Jackson and McNairy earned money by practicing law.

As he began his career as an attorney in Jonesborough, the twenty-one-year-old Jackson seemed more settled. He still enjoyed horse racing and cockfighting, like most gentlemen of the day, but he was becoming a respected attorney. His life now had direction.

Jackson was considered a gentleman, but he was still quick to lose his temper when insulted. Dueling was the accepted way to settle a fight between gentlemen, and Jackson soon issued his first challenge. Waightstill Avery, a man whom Jackson had always admired, was the attorney against Jackson in a court case. During the trial, Avery used sarcasm against Jackson to make his point. Jackson was angry when he left the courtroom and the next morning he issued Avery a formal challenge to duel. "When a man's feelings and charector [sic] are injured he ought to seek a speedy redress . . .," Jackson wrote. "I therefore call upon you as a gentleman to give me satisfaction for the Same. . . ."[3]

Neither Jackson nor Avery wanted to die over the issue, but the gentleman's code of honor said that an issued challenge had to be answered. Avery agreed to meet Jackson north of town shortly after sundown. The two men took their positions, fired their pistols into the air, shook hands, and called the matter settled.

Future slights would not be so easily settled, but the young Jackson had proved himself to be a gentleman of character and honor. He had also shown that he could compromise when he had to.

A few months later, Jackson and McNairy joined a group of settlers to complete their dangerous journey through the wilderness to Nashville. The party arrived in Nashville on October 26, 1788. Jackson found room and board at the widow Donelson's boardinghouse.

Rachel Donelson Robards, Widow Donelson's (also named Rachel) youngest daughter, had returned home and was also living at the boardinghouse. Jackson was attracted to Rachel from their first meeting. She was described as "the best story-teller, the best dancer, the sprightliest companion, the most dashing horsewoman in the western country."[4] She was also beautiful. An acquaintance described her "lustrous dark eyes" and claimed she was "irresistible to men," with her "beautifully moulded form, full red lips . . .," and face "rippling with smiles and dimples."[5]

Accounts vary concerning Jackson's behavior toward Rachel while he lived at the Donelsons'. Some said he baited Rachel's estranged husband Lewis Robards at every opportunity. Others said he was sympathetic to Rachel's plight but kept his distance. However, when Rachel grew frightened that Robards would bring her home by force, Jackson escorted her to Natchez, Mississippi, where she stayed with friends of his.[6] Robards finally declared the marriage over and stopped pursuing Rachel.

Jackson heard that Robards had applied for and won

a divorce. Without checking to see if this was true, Jackson married Rachel in Natchez, in August 1791. Two years after the marriage, in 1793, Jackson learned that Rachel's divorce had only then become final. To make their marriage official, the Jacksons married again on January 17, 1794.

Andrew and Rachel Jackson bought a 330-acre riverfront farm near Nashville, Tennessee, and began their life together as settlers on the frontier. Jackson's law practice prospered. He was paid largely in goods and land. He also bought land, so his holdings soon grew to thousands of acres. Jackson also made money in trading and other business ventures.

Soon after he and Rachel settled in Nashville, Andrew Jackson became a major player in frontier politics. His political career was helped along by his loyal support of the territorial governor, William Blount. In 1796, after Tennessee became a state, Jackson was elected by the legislature to serve as the state's first congressman. He served one term in the United States House of Representatives, then in 1798 he was elected to the United States Senate.

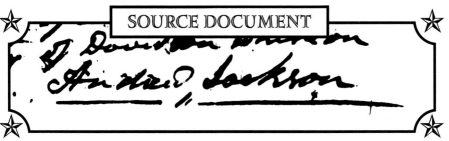

SOURCE DOCUMENT

This document shows Andrew Jackson's signature on a list of the slaves he owned.

By the time he was elected to the Senate, Jackson's fortunes had changed. Several land deals had failed when he could not collect money owed to him. Land deals were also foiled by President John Adams's failure to form key treaties with Native Americans. To make matters worse, Rachel did not like his frequent trips away from home.

For these reasons, Jackson was unable to keep his mind on his duties as senator. (He might also have been in awe of the more experienced politicians.) The young, inexperienced Jackson contributed little to Senate sessions in Philadelphia—at that time the nation's capital. In 1798, Jackson resigned his Senate seat and went home to Nashville.

After his short term as senator in 1798, Jackson was elected judge of the Superior Court of Tennessee. He was described as a strong, fair judge.

Jackson was proud of his work as a judge, but he had always wanted to be elected a major general in the militia. Earlier he had lost a bid for the position, but in 1802 he was elected. He ran for the position against his political enemy, John Sevier. Sevier was looking for a new job because he had served three terms as governor of Tennessee and, by state law, could serve no more. Jackson and Sevier each received seventeen votes. The tie was broken by the new governor of Tennessee, Archibald Roane. Governor Roane voted for his friend, Andrew Jackson.

At the age of thirty-five, Justice Jackson was now also Major General Jackson of the Tennessee militia.

In 1804, Jackson resigned his judgeship to devote more time to his failing businesses. He had taken promissory notes (written promises to pay, sometimes called IOUs), instead of cash, for some of the land he sold. He used the notes to buy more land and other purchases. When the original buyers did not pay off the notes, Jackson was left with debts he could not pay. Because of these bad debts, Jackson was nearly broke. To avoid bankruptcy, he sold off many acres of land, including the farm where he and Rachel lived. The Jacksons then bought a 420-acre farm near Nashville. They named their new home the Hermitage.

The Hermitage became a thriving plantation, and Jackson did not return to practicing law. For the first time since he and Rachel married, Jackson was at home for long periods of time. The couple longed for children, and in 1809 they adopted a nephew, the infant son of Elizabeth and Severn Donelson (Rachel Jackson's brother). The baby had a twin brother, and Elizabeth Donelson was too ill from childbirth to care for both infants. The Jacksons named the baby Andrew Jackson, Jr.

Another nephew, Andrew Donelson, also grew up in the Jackson home, but he was not formally adopted by them. In all, the Jacksons helped raise and educate at least eleven children, most of whom were offspring of Rachel's many relatives.[7]

By 1823, Jackson was again a fairly rich man. His wealth came through buying and selling land, farming, running a store, and racing a horse he owned.

Throughout his life, Jackson's hot temper often flared. Although he had challenged men to duels several times, most were not carried out. However, in 1806, an argument over a horse race turned into a duel in which Jackson killed twenty-seven-year-old Charles Dickinson.

When it was reported to Jackson that Dickinson had taken the "sacred name" of Rachel into his "polluted mouth," Jackson lost control.[8] Insults were traded through go-betweens, in letters, and in the local newspaper. (It was common at that time for men involved in a dispute to publish charges against one another in a newspaper.) Finally, Jackson issued a written challenge to Dickinson. The two men met on May 30, 1806, at a spot on the Red River in Kentucky, just over the state border from Nashville, Tennessee.

Local people saw the duel as a sporting event, and

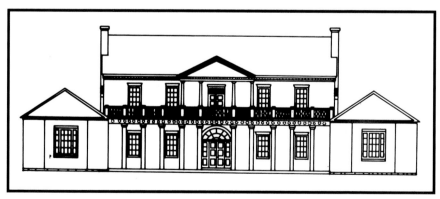

This drawing shows the Hermitage as it appeared when it was first built by the Jacksons.

they chose sides. Since Dickinson was said to be the best shot in Tennessee, most of the bets were placed on Dickinson to win and Jackson to lose.

On the day of the duel, the two men took their positions, eight paces apart. They strode in opposite directions, then turned to face each other. At the command to "fire," Dickinson raised his pistol and fired first. His bullet struck Jackson in the chest. Jackson wobbled but did not fall. Gritting his teeth in pain, he fired on Dickinson. Jackson's pistol misfired, but he drew back the hammer and fired on Dickinson again. This time the bullet struck Dickinson just beneath his ribs. Jackson's bullet passed through Dickinson's body. He lived for several hours but finally bled to death.

Because of a heavy, loose topcoat Jackson was wearing, Dickinson's bullet missed his heart. However, the bullet did much damage. It broke two of Jackson's ribs and lodged in his chest near his heart, where it would remain for the rest of his life.

Many thought that Jackson could have settled his dispute with Dickinson without bloodshed. Jackson was also criticized for firing on Dickinson again, after the first shot misfired. Therefore, after the duel, Jackson's hard-earned reputation as a gentleman and an honest person was at risk. For a while, Andrew Jackson was branded a violent, hateful man.

While it was true that Jackson had a fiery temper, those who knew him well claimed that his tantrums

Andrew and Rachel Jackson adopted a nephew in 1809. This portrait shows Andrew Jackson, Jr., at about eleven years of age.

were sometimes faked, in order to get rivals to do what he wanted. In *The Revolutionary Age of Andrew Jackson*, historian Robert V. Remini quotes a man who knew Jackson: "No man knew better than Andrew Jackson when to get into a passion and when not."[9]

It was also true that Jackson was ambitious, but in public life his concern was mainly for the country. He believed strongly in westward growth and in the freedom to seek one's fortune. These were two strong American goals that had come out of the colonial era. More than any other man of his time, Andrew Jackson worked on making those goals possible. To do this, he fought the Spanish, the British, and the Native Americans.

4

OLD HICKORY

A ndrew Jackson had little military experience when he became major general of the Tennessee militia in 1802. Still, the general was known for his stubborn loyalty to friends and country, and the soldiers under his command trusted him.

Ten years after being elected major general, Jackson had not yet been called to duty. He had offered his services whenever the country was threatened. However, each time he thought he would be called to lead men into battle, the conflict was settled without fighting. Then in 1812, the United States declared war against Great Britain.

The declaration of war did not come suddenly or without cause. The Treaty of Paris in 1783 had officially ended the American Revolution, but it did not end

England's attacks on America. Great Britain continued to take American ships, to kidnap American sailors for service to the king, and to goad Native Americans into attacking settlers. Moreover, since Canada was a British territory, Americans worried that the British would come down from the north and try to conquer them. Adding to the strain was the fact that Spain held a large area in the southeastern United States called the Floridas. Britain and Spain were allies and Americans knew they would side together if war broke out.

Serving in Congress at this time were several members of the Democratic-Republican party who wanted to declare war against Great Britain. A victory, they said, would open up expansion, creating an America that stretched from ocean to ocean. This group of "War Hawks" included South Carolina's John C. Calhoun, William Lowndes, and Langdon Cheves; Richard M. Johnson and Henry Clay of Kentucky; Peter B. Porter of New York; and Tennessee's Felix Grundy and John Sevier.[1]

The War Hawks kept hammering away at other members of Congress, trying to convince them to fight Great Britain. Since Henry Clay was speaker of the House of Representatives, he was especially powerful. In June 1812, the War Hawks got their way. Congress declared war on Great Britain.

Once the war began, Jackson was eager to lead his troops into battle. Other generals were given assignments that he felt should have been his. When

Native Americans joined with the British to fight against the American militia, William Henry Harrison was sent. He led the Indiana and Kentucky militias in an attack against the Shawnee chief, Tecumseh. Harrison was successful, but other American officers were not. Henry Dearborn led a failed attack against Canada. General William Hull surrendered Detroit, without a shot, to an army of Native American and British soldiers.

Although the war was going badly for the Americans, Jackson still waited at the Hermitage for an assignment. Jackson thought that an earlier friendship with Aaron Burr was keeping him from battle and he was probably right. Burr had killed Alexander Hamilton in a duel. Later he was charged with treason against the United States for plotting to conquer Mexico and divide the Union. Jackson had denounced Burr's scheme as soon as he learned what was going on, but he had agreed to testify for Burr at his trial. Though Burr was found not guilty of treason, Jackson's reputation was tainted by his friendship with Burr.

Finally, Jackson's call to battle came. Governor Blount of Tennessee, his old friend, made him a commander of United States volunteers. He was ordered by the United States War Department to take his troops to New Orleans, Louisiana. New Orleans was a vital port city that America could not afford to lose to the British.

Jackson would have been happy about this long-overdue call to action except that his commanding officer was a man he hated, General James Wilkinson.

John C. Calhoun was one of the War Hawks who pushed for war with Great Britain. He would later serve as Vice President under Andrew Jackson.

Wilkinson, a suspected spy for the Spanish, had plotted with Burr, then later denied any part in Burr's plan. Jackson considered him a traitor and a coward.

In January 1813, Jackson and the twenty-five hundred volunteers under his command sailed down the Cumberland, Ohio, and Mississippi Rivers to Natchez, Mississippi. The plan was to sail on to New Orleans, then wait for further orders from President James Madison.

Thirty-nine days after leaving Nashville, Jackson and his troops arrived in Natchez. Several letters from General Wilkinson in New Orleans were there waiting for him. Jackson was to stay in Natchez, Wilkinson ordered, since there were no extra supplies in New Orleans to share with new troops.

Jackson's troops camped four miles from Natchez. Weeks passed while they awaited further orders. Finally, on March 15, 1813, Jackson received an order from Secretary of War John Armstrong to dismiss his men and send them home.

Supplies had long ago run out and Jackson's men were ragged, cold, and hungry. Because of their living conditions, some were sick. Jackson refused to dismiss them to find their own way home. Instead, he borrowed money for wagons and supplies for his troops and marched with them back to Tennessee. It was during the long march home that Jackson's men dubbed him "Old Hickory." Because hickory was the strongest of the hardwoods, the soldiers thought the nickname a suitable tribute to their general's toughness and courage.

At home, word of Jackson's kind treatment of his men made him a hero. "Long will their General live in the memory of his volunteers of West Tennessee," said a newspaper called the *Nashville Whig*, "for his benevolence, humane, and fatherly treatment to his soldiers; if gratitude and love can reward him, General Jackson has them."[2] Although Jackson's reputation had never been better, his temper again caused trouble. During the march home from Natchez, Jackson had seemed to favor his brigade inspector, William Carroll. Other officers were jealous of Jackson's fondness for Carroll, and a quarrel broke out between Carroll and Littleton Johnston, another officer.

Johnston challenged Carroll to a duel, but Carroll refused to fight on the grounds that Johnston was not a gentleman. Carroll insisted that he only fought gentlemen. Refusing to give up, Johnston asked Jesse Benton, who was considered a gentleman in social circles, to carry the challenge. (Jesse Benton was the brother of Thomas Hart Benton, Jackson's military aide and friend.)

Carroll could not refuse without being called a coward, so he accepted the challenge. He asked Jackson to be his second in the duel. (Each duelist chose a second to help and support him.) At first Jackson refused, but then he agreed to ride with Carroll to Nashville, to "inquire into this business myself."[3] Jackson tried, but failed to talk the two men out of the duel. He finally agreed to serve as Carroll's second.

The duel was held on June 14, 1813. Carroll was shot in the thumb. The unfortunate Benton was wounded in the seat of the pants.

A few weeks later Thomas Hart Benton heard of his brother's disgrace. He blamed Andrew Jackson for not stopping the fight, and swore to get even. Jackson heard of Benton's insults and threatened to horsewhip him on sight.

In September, the threats and insults between Benton and Jackson finally erupted into a gunfight. By chance, Jackson and his friend, John Coffee, met the two Benton brothers on a Nashville street. Jackson again threatened to horsewhip Thomas Benton, and raised his whip as if to do so.

In the fight that followed, Jesse Benton fired at Jackson's back, hitting him in the arm and shoulder. After a scuffle, Coffee and several bystanders ended the fight. They carried Jackson to the Nashville Inn, then sent for a doctor. Jackson refused to let surgeons amputate his arm. He lost so much blood that he could not get out of bed for three weeks. Like the bullet in his chest, Jackson would carry the shot in his shoulder for the rest of his life.

In October 1813, while still weak from his wound, Jackson was ordered to put down a Creek uprising in Mississippi Territory. The Spanish in Florida had encouraged the Creek revolt, promising to give the

Native Americans arms and supplies. Shawnee Chief Tecumseh, who was friendly with the Creeks, and Chief Red Eagle (also known as William Weatherford), leader of the Creeks, led their people against Jackson and his troops.

While Tecumseh and Chief Red Eagle urged their warriors to fight, other Creek leaders wanted peace. This division within the Creek nation led to inner discord that Jackson was able to use. Hundreds of Native Americans were killed in several bloody battles where Jackson's troops vastly outnumbered the Creeks.

During the war, supplies for Jackson's troops ran out. Many times the hungry soldiers threatened to mutiny. To make matters worse, Jackson was in constant pain from his wounded shoulder. He was also ill from hunger and dysentery (a disease that causes severe diarrhea). Barely able to sit on his horse, Jackson had to struggle to hold his army together.

As usual, Old Hickory showed that he could be kind as well as cruel. When his men found a Creek baby crying beside his dead mother, Jackson ordered the infant sent home to Rachel. The orphaned baby, named Lyncoya by the Jacksons, would be raised with their adopted son, Andrew, Jr. (Lyncoya lived with the Jacksons until he died of tuberculosis at the age of seventeen.)

On the other hand, when his troops were deserting and Jackson had to restore order, he showed no mercy. At one point Jackson stood in the way of men fleeing

This portrait, done around 1818, shows the young, dashing Andrew Jackson in his military uniform.

the battlefield, threatening to shoot them himself if they did not go back. In another incident, John Woods, a young recruit had been caught away from his post. Woods swore that he had permission to leave his post to get a blanket from his tent. When Woods refused to be arrested, Jackson made an example of him by ordering his court-martial and execution. The event put an end to desertion, but it haunted Jackson later, when he campaigned for President.

Finally, at the Battle of Horseshoe Bend in March 1814, in present-day Alabama, the outnumbered Creeks fought to the end but lost. After his victory, Jackson imposed a cruel treaty called the Treaty of Fort Jackson. The treaty took most of the Native Americans' land away from them, effectively destroying the Creek nation.

The weary Native American leaders who suffered through the one-sided talks with Jackson dubbed him "Sharp Knife."[4] Since most of the hostile chiefs had been killed in the fighting, those who signed the final treaty with Jackson were actually friendly to the United States government.

After his victory over the Creeks, Jackson was again called a hero. He was promoted to major general in the United States Army. He would command troops from Tennessee and South Carolina to the Gulf of Mexico, including Louisiana, Alabama, and Mississippi.

Although Jackson had won a victory over the Creeks in less than eighteen months, on other fronts the War of 1812 was not going well. On August 24, 1814, while

President Madison was out reviewing American troops, the British marched on Washington, D.C. Fortunately, First Lady Dolley Madison had already fled the White House when British soldiers burned it and the Capitol Building.

The British then began planning a huge invasion from the Gulf of Mexico that would drive Americans out of Florida, Louisiana, Mississippi, and Alabama. Alarmed by reports from spies, Jackson moved five hundred regular army troops to Mobile, Alabama, arriving on August 22, 1814. From Mobile, Jackson learned that British troops had come ashore at Pensacola, Florida, with the cooperation of Spanish Governor Don Matteo Gonzalez Manrique. The word was that British marines had occupied Fort Barrancas and were training one thousand Native Americans to fight. Ten thousand more British troops were expected to march on Mobile.

Although President Madison was hesitant to order Jackson to invade Spanish-held territory, Old Hickory urged him to do so at once. On November 2, "without the orders of the government," Jackson led his soldiers to Pensacola, Florida, where he demanded the surrender of the city and nearby forts.[5] Governor Manrique waved a white flag of surrender and welcomed Jackson into his home, assuring him that the forts would also be surrendered. The Creek and Seminole warriors who were training with the British deserted them. The British burned Fort Barrancas and sailed away.

Jackson led a hurried march back to Mobile, which

had been left unprotected during the trip to Florida. He then left Mobile for New Orleans. On December 2, 1814, a tired General Jackson and an advance staff of six or eight riders arrived in New Orleans.

Jackson's health had been poor since the Benton incident. He was in constant pain from old wounds and had chronic dysentery. A merchant who entertained Jackson's party when they reached New Orleans described him as

> a tall, gaunt man, of very erect carriage, with a countenance full of stern decision and fearless energy, but furrowed with care and anxiety. . . . His complexion was sallow and unhealthy; his hair iron grey, his body thin and emaciated. . . . But the fierce glare of his bright and hawk-like grey eye, betrayed a soul and spirit which triumphed over all the infirmities of the body.[6]

At times too ill to stand, Jackson took charge of getting New Orleans ready for the coming British invasion. On December 16, he put the city under martial law, which meant that no one could enter or leave without the general's permission. Street lights went out at 9:00 P.M., and a strict curfew was enforced. By December 23, when the British were spotted near New Orleans, Jackson had gathered thirty-five hundred fighting men.[7]

A strange mixture of men came to fight under Old Hickory in the swamps around New Orleans. There were riflemen and horsemen from Tennessee, Mississippi, Alabama, and Louisiana. A band of Choctaw scouts was there, led by Pierre Jugeat, whose father was

French and mother was Native American. A group of Creoles ran all the way to New Orleans from Fort St. John on Lake Pontchartrain to join in the battle. A company of New Orleans riflemen included lawyers, notaries, and court clerks. The pirate chief Jean Laffite and his brother, Pierre, sent men, ships, and cannons for the fight. (Laffite's pirates helped more in Jackson's eventual victory at New Orleans than the general or history gave them credit for.)

Jackson's backwoods fighters were good at slipping through tangled underbrush and creeping quietly through knee-deep water to surprise the enemy. They also waited behind barricades to destroy marching walls of red-coated enemy soldiers. In the end, they proved better able to fight in the Louisiana swamps than the rigid-ranked British military.

Fierce battles were fought and won by the Americans that January of 1815. After a major battle on January 8, American forces counted only seventy-one dead and wounded, while the British suffered nearly two thousand casualties. General Sir Edward Pakenham, commander of the British forces, was among the 289 British dead.[8]

By the night of January 18, the British army was in full retreat. By mid-February 1815, President Madison received word that the Treaty of Ghent, Belgium, had been signed, ending the War of 1812. (The treaty had actually been signed before the Battle of New Orleans, but it took several weeks for the news to reach

America.) As news of the truce spread, Andrew Jackson was again the nation's hero. "If we had a Jackson everywhere we should succeed everywhere," said the *New York Evening Post.*[9]

In 1818, Jackson was again ordered to Florida, to drive out the Seminoles who were hunting in Georgia, in violation of the Fort Jackson treaty. At that time, he ordered the execution of Robert Ambrister and Alexander Arbuthnot. The two were English citizens who had earlier been tried and found guilty of aiding the Seminoles. This act again caused critics to label Jackson a cruel, vindictive man.

Whatever critics said of his methods, Jackson was effective, as usual. His final march helped bring about the Adams-Onis Treaty (Florida Purchase Treaty) of 1819, wherein the Spanish gave up all claims to the Florida Territory.

Jackson was exhausted and ill after his military duty. In fact, he would never be entirely healthy again. Nevertheless, he served a short term as governor of the Florida Territory before he and Rachel went home to the Hermitage.

Jackson's victories in the War of 1812 opened up new territory for settlers—land taken from the British, the Spanish, and Native Americans. Old Hickory's successes on the battlefield also won him attention that would help when he later ran for President of the United States.

5

JACKSON AND REFORM

R achel Jackson wanted to live quietly at the Hermitage, but Andrew Jackson was too politically ambitious to retire from public life. His friends and supporters urged him to run for President. Jackson felt he was ready for the job.

In 1822, the Tennessee legislature nominated Jackson to run for President. However, some of his supporters feared that they might not have enough political power to get Jackson elected President. Therefore, they entered his name as a candidate for the United States Senate.

Although he had not sought the job and did not want it, Jackson won the 1823 Senate race. He again left the Hermitage and traveled to Washington, D.C. Old Hickory, the war hero, United States senator, and candidate for President, was well received in Washington. As the center of national attention, he knew he had to keep his famous temper under control, or suffer disgrace. "When it becomes necessary to philosophise & be meek," he wrote, "no man can command his temper better than I."[1]

Jackson not only controlled his temper, he behaved with dignity and charm. He was soon sought after in both social and political circles. Unlike his brief term as a senator in 1798, he paid close attention to his duties. This time, Senator Jackson served with honor as a member of the Foreign Relations Committee and as chairman of the Committee on Military Affairs.

Senator Jackson settled a number of old quarrels, including his spat with Thomas Hart Benton. Benton was also a member of the Senate and the two men often went to the same committee meetings and social functions. When they met, they spoke politely to one another and shook hands. Soon Jackson and Benton picked up the friendship that had been cut short ten years before. In the future, Benton would prove a major political ally in Jackson's bid for the presidency.

As the 1824 election drew near, four candidates were in the running for President: William H. Crawford, John Quincy Adams, Henry Clay, and Andrew Jackson. Crawford was the last presidential candidate ever to be chosen by congressional caucus. (A caucus was a closed meeting held by members of Congress to choose

Despite early problems between them, Thomas Hart Benton became a good friend and strong supporter of Andrew Jackson.

candidates to run for President.) Adams, Clay, and Jackson had been nominated by their home states.

Jackson had two advantages over the other candidates. First, he was the "Hero of New Orleans." Second, he was a member of the militia, like nearly every other voting American male. These advantages paid off. When votes were counted, Andrew Jackson was the people's choice. He received 155,800 votes. Next in line were Adams with 105,300 votes, Clay with 46,500 votes, and Crawford with 44,200 votes.[2]

Electoral votes in the 1824 election also favored Jackson, but he did not win a majority. No candidate received a majority of the electoral votes. Andrew Jackson won 99 electoral votes. John Quincy Adams received 84; William H. Crawford, 41; and Henry Clay, 37.[3] Therefore, the House of Representatives chose the President, as required by the United States Constitution.

Since he received the fewest electoral votes, Clay was removed from the race at once. As a member of the House, Clay then used his influence to sway the vote toward John Quincy Adams. Adams had reportedly promised Clay the job of secretary of state, if he would help him get elected President.

John Quincy Adams won the election in the House of Representatives, to become the sixth President of the United States. Five days later, Adams appointed Henry Clay secretary of state.

Jackson's campaign pledge was to reform the government and get rid of corruption. He and his supporters made much of the "corrupt bargain" that had won Adams the presidency. "I weep for the Liberty of my country," Jackson wrote. The "rights of the people have been bartered for promises of office."[4]

From the day Adams took office, Jackson supporters began preparing for him to run for President in 1828. Jackson's side used two points to build support for him: the deal between Clay and Adams, and the fact that the will of the people had been ignored in the election. Since the voters clearly chose him, Jackson should have been elected, they said. If government could so easily be stolen from the people, then liberty itself was in danger.

A strong base of support for Jackson was built within the Democratic-Republican party. (The name "Democratic-Republican" was first used in the 1790s to describe Thomas Jefferson and his political views. The party became the Democratic party after 1828.) Jackson became his party's leader. The party nominated him for President in the election of 1828. The National Republicans (the Whig party in the 1830s) opposed Jackson and nominated President John Quincy Adams to run against him.

The campaign of 1828 was the most brutal in American history to that point. Jackson was called a murderer for his duel with Dickinson. He was also criticized for his order to execute six militiamen for desertion. He was accused of land fraud and treason in the Burr incident. Critics also said he had ignored the nation's laws and Constitution. They cited events in

This is Andrew Jackson, the Tennessee gentleman, as he appeared shortly before he was elected President.

Florida that took place while he was governor, when he suspended the writ of *habeas corpus* and ordered a judge jailed. (The right of *habeas corpus* is guaranteed by Article I, Section 9 of the United States Constitution. The term is Latin for "[that] you have the body." It is a court order that says that a jailer must bring a prisoner to court for a judgment on whether or not imprisonment is legal.)

As discussed earlier, charges were also made about the Jacksons' marriage. This probably contributed to Rachel's death on December 22, 1828.

In spite of the attacks made by his opponents, Jackson won the 1828 presidential election by a landslide. He received 178 electoral votes to incumbent President John Quincy Adams's 83. John C. Calhoun was elected Vice President.[5]

When President Jackson arrived in Washington, he began at once to choose his cabinet members. He appointed his old friend and campaign advisor, Senator John Eaton from Tennessee, as secretary of war. Martin Van Buren was made secretary of state. Other cabinet members were Samuel D. Ingham, secretary of the treasury; John Branch, secretary of the navy; John M. Berrien, attorney general; and William T. Barry, postmaster general.

Jackson also gave government positions to his old friends John Overton, John Coffee, and William Lewis. In addition, newspaper editors Amos Kendall, Isaac Hill, and Francis Blair were hired to produce *The Globe*, a newspaper that promoted the President's causes. This group of Jackson appointees advised the President but were not official members of the cabinet. They were called the "Kitchen Cabinet," because they supposedly met in the White House kitchen.

President Jackson consulted the Kitchen Cabinet more often than he assembled his official cabinet. In fact, during his first two years in office, Jackson did not once meet with his cabinet. He called cabinet meetings only sixteen times during his eight years in office. "I have accustomed myself to receive with respect the opinions of others, but always take the responsibility for deciding for myself," Jackson explained.[6]

This political cartoon shows Jackson as a demon, flying above office seekers, offering them political plums. The office seekers twist and grab at the offered electoral spoils.

The official cabinet member President Jackson called upon most for advice was his secretary of state, Martin Van Buren. Except for their political beliefs, the two men were opposites. Jackson was tall and thin; Van Buren was short and stout. Jackson stormed, argued, and lost his temper in a debate. Van Buren spoke softly and was a master of political compromise, for which he earned the nickname "The Little Magician." However, shared political goals made the two men friends throughout Jackson's presidency. After he left office, Jackson pushed for Van Buren's nomination for President.

Jackson's first major problem after becoming President had little to do with national or foreign affairs, but concerned one of his cabinet members. Secretary of War John Eaton married a local innkeeper's daughter, Peggy O'Neale. Mrs. Eaton had been the subject of gossip for her flirtatious behavior while married to her first husband. Other cabinet members and their wives refused to have anything to do with her. (This included Jackson's niece, Emily Donelson.)

Jackson defended Mrs. Eaton, perhaps because he remembered all too well the abuse suffered by his beloved Rachel. He was kind to Mrs. Eaton and refused to give in to those who urged him to settle the matter by firing her husband. At one point Jackson remarked, "I would resign the presidency sooner than desert my friend Eaton."[7]

The problem was finally solved by a suggestion from

Emily Donelson, who often served as her Uncle Andrew Jackson's White House hostess, was among those who disapproved of Mrs. Peggy Eaton.

Martin Van Buren. He proposed that all the cabinet members resign and be given new jobs. Jackson took Van Buren's advice and gave Eaton a new job away from Washington. Only then did the business of running the government resume.

Some historians claim that the Eaton flap, resulting in a cabinet overhaul, was caused by Vice President John C. Calhoun. Calhoun wanted to follow Jackson as President, but Jackson's choice for the next President was Secretary of State Martin Van Buren. Calhoun may have thought that if he could force Van Buren to quit, he would have a better chance of someday becoming President.

Van Buren resigned with other cabinet members to help settle the Eaton matter. Still, Jackson remained loyal to Van Buren. Calhoun tried to get even. When Jackson later nominated Van Buren as minister to Great Britain, Vice President Calhoun broke a tie for Senate confirmation by voting against Van Buren. Calhoun's act effectively ended his political influence within the Democratic party. It also ended any hope Calhoun had of becoming President.

After the Eaton matter was settled, Jackson began work in earnest. During his first term as President, he worked on many issues that had long concerned him. For instance, difficulties with the Native Americans continued. As always, the dispute was over land that the settlers wanted. Jackson was criticized for pushing the Native Americans off their land, but he did not soften

Peggy Eaton was at the center of Jackson's first major controversy as President. Though Mrs. Eaton was the subject of much gossip because of her flirtatious manners, Jackson defended her and kept her husband, John, as his secretary of war.

his position. He proposed setting aside certain western lands for Native Americans who were removed from their homes east of the Mississippi. Jackson was so strongly in favor of American expansion that he believed confining Native Americans to reservations was best for them and for the country.

President Jackson also called for ending the electoral college. Based upon his own experience in 1824, he believed the electoral system had stolen from the people their right to elect the presidential candidate of their choice. (Jackson did not succeed. The electoral college system of electing the President and Vice President has continued to the present day.)

In addition, Jackson called for rotation of government jobs. Appointees should not continue to hold their jobs from one President's term in office to the next, he said. "There are, perhaps, few who can for any length of time enjoy office and power without being more or less under the influence of feelings unfavorable to the faithful discharge of their public duties."[8] Not only did rotation prevent dishonesty, it also meant increased efficiency and cooperation within an administration. He proposed term limits of four years for government officials. However, in President Jackson's two terms in office, no more than one fifth of all federal officeholders were removed.[9]

One of President Jackson's most important goals was to pay off the national debt. In his first message to Congress in December 1829, he said that the government had a surplus of money, thanks to sales of public lands. Therefore, the national debt would be reduced to $48.5 million within a year's time. Jackson accurately predicted that the entire debt would soon be repaid.

During his first term in office, President Jackson told

SOURCE DOCUMENT

To the Senate & House of Representatives

Washington, April 2. 1834.

I lay before Congress a Communication from the Governor of New Jersey and a copy of a communication from the Governor of New York, addressed to me with the view of obtaining the consent of Congress to an Agreement which has been entered into by the States of New York and New Jersey, to settle the Boundary Line between those States. The Agreement, and authenticated copies of the Acts of the Legislatures of New York and New Jersey relating to it, are also transmitted.

Andrew Jackson

Among the jobs President Jackson was called upon to handle was the settlement of a boundary dispute between New York and New Jersey, the subject of this letter.

Congress that he was against continuing the Second Bank of the United States. He believed the bank was too powerful, was less safe than smaller state banks, and was a corrupt influence.

The Second Bank of the United States was a private bank that had been formed in 1816 for the purpose of keeping the federal government's money. Its charter allowed it to keep the government's funds for twenty years. Jackson was against the bank because frontier settlers and farmers had been hurt by its high interest rates. Jackson also believed rumors that the bank had illegally released information about him during his presidential campaign. Therefore, President Jackson did not want the bank's charter to be renewed when it expired in 1836.

Andrew Jackson's first term as President marked many firsts for American government. As the people's choice, he was the first "populist," or people's President. Jackson was a popular hero, and when he was elected, Americans became more interested in the government and its affairs than ever before.

Old Hickory, the hero of the War of 1812, used his popularity with the public to sway Congress to agree with his views. President Jackson did not give in to Congress when decisions had to be made. Instead, he used his power of the veto, his party leadership, and his popularity to fulfill his goals.

Andrew Jackson began the practice among Presidents of appealing directly to the people for support. As an opponent of banking and big business interests, he was considered a friend to veterans, settlers, frontiersmen, and farmers. When he finished his first term in office at sixty-six years of age, Andrew Jackson was still popular with the people who had elected him.

6

A LANDSLIDE IN 1832

B y the time Andrew Jackson ran for reelection in 1832, the method of choosing presidential candidates had changed. Congressional caucuses and state legislatures no longer chose candidates. For the first time in history, candidates for President and Vice President were nominated by national political conventions. This practice continues today.

The Democrats and Republicans hold separate conventions. Each state chooses delegates to go to the national conventions, usually held during the summer in an election year. The convention delegates vote on candidates to run for President and Vice President. The candidates who get a majority of the vote are nominated.

At the 1832 Democratic National Convention,

Andrew Jackson was nominated for President, with Martin Van Buren as Vice President. The National Republican party chose Henry Clay. In the election, Jackson received 56 percent of the popular vote. He won 219 electoral votes to Clay's 49. Minor candidates received a total of 18 electoral votes.[1]

Some of the problems that began during Jackson's first term continued in his second. For instance, before his first term ended, Vice President John C. Calhoun started a dispute that could have led to civil war. The clash began in 1828, when Congress passed a high tax bill. Calhoun's native state, South Carolina, led the South in protesting the bill. The law placed a high tax on goods coming into America. New England states favored the tax, because it meant people would buy goods made in factories in New England, instead of the higher-priced imported goods. The Southern states wanted a low tax, because they traded cotton for imported goods. A high tax meant they would lose in the exchange.

The debate grew. The question became: Which is more important to liberty, states' rights or the laws of the federal government? Calhoun argued on the side of states' rights. He claimed that the Union was merely a collection of states and that the individual states were more important. He said that when a state did not agree with a federal law, the state should nullify that law—declare the law void within its borders. If the federal government refused to allow a state to nullify its laws,

SOURCE DOCUMENT

Washington
January 6th 1834

To the Senate of
the United States

I communicate to Congress an
extract of a letter recently received from J
R Leib, Consul of the U States at
Tangier, by which it appears that, that officer
has been induced to receive from the Emperor
of Morocco a present of a Lion and two
horses, which he holds as belonging to the
U States. There being no funds at the
disposal of the Executive applicable to the
objects stated by Mr Leib, I submit the
whole subject to the consideration of Congress
for such direction as in their wisdom
may seem proper.

In this letter, Jackson gives his recommendations to the Senate on a
question about what to do with a lion and two horses that the United
States Consul at Tangier received as gifts from the Emperor of Morocco.

then that state could secede, or withdraw from the Union.

Jackson respected states' rights, but he believed America's future depended upon preserving the Union. To do that, federal law would have to come first, before the laws passed in each state. No state should have the right to secede.

Old Hickory responded to Calhoun's nullification idea in his usual manner. He told a South Carolina congressman to deliver this message to his state, "if a single drop of blood shall be shed there in opposition to the laws of the United States, I will hang the first man I can lay my hand on engaged in such treasonable conduct, upon the first tree I can reach."[2]

Thomas Hart Benton, Jackson's friend who had once been an enemy, knew the President meant what he said. "If Andrew Jackson starts talking about hanging people, you better go out and find some rope," said Benton.[3]

Jackson would not be reinaugurated until March 4, 1833, but one of his first acts after he was reelected was to issue a proclamation (statement) to the people of South Carolina. In his proclamation, dated December 10, 1832, Jackson listed his views of the Constitution. He explained that the states did not and could not have the right to secede from the Union. He said that citizens of a state were first American citizens and owed obedience to the Constitution and to federal laws.

Jackson also warned the people of South Carolina

that as President he was sworn to uphold the Constitution and federal law. He said that he would use military force if necessary. "Disunion by armed force is treason," he said.[4]

When he heard that South Carolina had called for volunteers to resist the federal government, Jackson remarked, "If South Carolina raises an army of twelve thousand men, I will order thirty thousand to execute the law."[5]

Although Jackson was known for his hot temper, he had learned how to compromise. A new tariff had been passed in 1832, which lowered some taxes. In January 1833, a bill was introduced in Congress that provided for further reductions in the tariff. That same month the Force Bill was passed, allowing President Jackson to use force to collect taxes when necessary. Jackson signed both bills on March 2, 1833.

Nullifiers in South Carolina were pleased with the new tax schedule and dropped nullification action. (In an attempt to have the last word, South Carolina nullified the Force Bill.) In putting down South Carolina's threat to secede, Jackson was credited with preventing civil war. He predicted, however, that a clash between the North and the South over slavery would come at some later date. "The South intends to blow up a storm on the slave question," he said. "This ought to be met, for be assured these men would do any act to destroy this Union and form a southern confederacy."[6]

As Jackson had foretold, a bloody civil war between

the North and the South broke out some twenty-eight years later, under President Abraham Lincoln. At that time, South Carolina would lead the South in seceding from the Union.

After the nullification matter was settled, John C. Calhoun resigned as Vice President, two months before the end of his term. South Carolina then elected him to Congress. He would spend the rest of his days in Congress defending slavery in South Carolina. He would never again be in line for President.

The chief issue of Jackson's second presidential campaign was the Second Bank of the United States. Chartered in 1816, the bank kept the federal government's money. In 1832, President Jackson vetoed a bill to renew the bank's charter when it ran out in 1836, but the bank continued to operate until that date.

In March 1832, the government tried to withdraw a large sum of money from the Second Bank of the United States to pay off the national debt. The bank did not have that much cash on hand, so the bank's president, Nicholas Biddle, planned to get the money from foreign investors. Biddle's plan violated the bank's charter and President Jackson called for an investigation by the House Ways and Means Committee. Jackson hoped to show corruption in the bank's dealings. He wanted to withdraw all government funds and close the bank for good.

After a three-week probe, the investigating committee decided that government deposits were safe with the Second Bank of the United States. Jackson started his own investigation. He called one of his few cabinet meetings to discuss the matter. At the meeting, he pushed for immediate withdrawal of all government funds from the bank. Jackson's plan was to move the funds to several state banks—so-called pet banks—that had agreed to take them. Secretary of the Treasury William Duane was against taking such action without the approval of Congress.

Duane refused to follow Jackson's order to withdraw government funds from the Second Bank of the United States. He also refused to resign. This raised a question that had not yet come up for a President. The Constitution states that cabinet appointments must be approved by the Senate. Could a President fire one of his cabinet members without the consent of the Senate? Earlier Presidents had not faced the problem, because when there was a disagreement, cabinet members had simply resigned.

Jackson boldly attacked the problem. Cabinet members worked for him, not Congress, he said, and they should take orders from him. In a short note, dated September 23, 1833, Jackson told Duane that "your further services as Secretary of the Treasury are no longer required."[7]

Jackson appointed Roger Brooke Taney, his attorney general, to replace Duane at the Treasury. (Taney's appointment was rejected by the Senate and he was replaced by Levi Woodbury.) The Second Bank of the

Washington
December 28.ᵗ 1835

To the Senate

I nominate — Roger B Taney Esq.
of Maryland to be chief Justice of the
Supreme Court of the United States in the
place of John Marshall deceased : and
Philip P Barbour Esq. of Virginia to be
Associate Justice of the same court in the
place of Gabriel Duval resigned.

Andrew Jackson

Jackson tried to appoint Roger B. Taney to the Treasury in 1833. In
this December 28, 1835, letter, Jackson nominated Taney as Chief
Justice of the Supreme Court.

Old Hickory looks his age in this portrait, painted by Ralph E. Earl around 1833.

United States was notified that no more government deposits would be made after September 1833.

Bank President Biddle hoped to sway Congress in favor of the bank by making people suffer. Interest rates went up and private loans were called in. Businesses failed, jobs were lost, and many people turned against Jackson. Old Hickory refused to budge. "I will not bow down to the golden calf," he vowed.[8]

Senator Henry Clay introduced a resolution to censure (scold) Jackson for "unconstitutional" acts. The resolution was passed, but still Jackson would not give in. He protested the censure and continued his attack against the Second Bank of the United States. When Biddle would not ease conditions, the public turned against the bank, instead of Jackson. Congress then passed resolutions against rechartering the bank and against restoring the deposits. The charter for the Second Bank of the United States ran out in 1836. It then received a state charter as the United States Bank of Pennsylvania, but it was no longer a federal institution. In 1841, it declared bankruptcy.

President Jackson also used his power boldly in issuing the Specie Circular on July 11, 1836. As settlers moved to the West in the 1800s, land sales exploded. State banks were accepting "land office money," which was paper based on land speculators' notes, or written promises to pay. These notes were usually backed only by former land purchases. This practice led to inflated land prices. Because the currency that was used to buy land was not based on something of fixed value, like gold or silver, inflation ran wild.

Jackson feared that runaway land speculation and the resulting inflation would cause the economy to crash. To prevent this, he issued an executive order called the Specie Circular. This order said that only specie (gold or silver) could be used to buy public land. Jackson issued his order while Congress was adjourned, because he was afraid they would pass a law to cancel it.

Land speculators, bankers, and Whigs did not like the Specie Circular. Ordinary working people praised it. However, Jackson's order put a strain on banks that led to more inflation and land speculation. Congress passed a law canceling the Specie Circular, which President Jackson pocket-vetoed just before he left office in March

SOURCE DOCUMENT

There are no necessary evils in government. Its evils exist only in its abuses. If it would confine itself to equal protection and, as Heaven does its rains, shower its favors alike on the high and the low, the rich and the poor, it would be an unqualified blessing.

(Message to Congress vetoing the renewal of the charter of the Second Bank of the United States, July 10, 1832)

In this 1832 message to Congress vetoing the charter of the Second Bank of the United States, Jackson discusses his ideal for the operation of government.

1837. (If the President does not sign or veto a bill, it automatically becomes law after ten days. A pocket veto occurs if the President does nothing and Congress adjourns before the ten-day time limit is up.)

In 1837, a financial panic struck. Andrew Jackson's money measures had contributed to the crash. By destroying the Second Bank of the United States, he had removed all checks upon inflationary practices of some state banks. Land speculation increased, based on easy bank credit throughout the West. The depression lasted for the next five years, during President Martin Van Buren's presidency. Van Buren continued Andrew Jackson's monetary policies, which added to the depression.

During his second term, Jackson continued his practice of removing all Native Americans from land east of the Mississippi River. He signed more than ninety removal treaties, promising Native Americans land in the West that they could keep "forever." However, by the time he left office in 1837, almost every one of the Native American treaties had been broken. The government forced thousands of Creeks, Choctaws, Cherokees, and Seminoles to give up their homes and march westward.

One of the most inhuman acts resulting from Jackson's removal policy was the Trail of Tears in 1838. In this forced eight-hundred-mile march of fifteen thousand Cherokees, more than four thousand died.[9] Jackson had left office by the time the march occurred, but his harsh removal policy for Native Americans was widely criticized. His passion for expansion—for opening up more land to settlers—guided his actions. Yet the cruel way he dealt with the nation's Native Americans cost many of them their lives. Furthermore, thousands of survivors lost their homeland and their way of life.

One of President Jackson's chief goals was to pay off the national debt. Congress had voted to assume the states' debt of $25 million after the American Revolution. The national debt increased again with the War of 1812. When President Jackson took office it had grown to $45 million.

During Jackson's second term, the government made money from sales of land in the West and from taxes on foreign trade. In addition, by using American ships to back up his demands, Jackson was able to collect United States government claims against foreign nations totaling more than $12 million. As a result, the government made more money than it spent. On January 8, 1835, Jackson used the surplus to pay off the national debt, as he had promised in his first annual message to Congress in 1829. For the first and last time in American history to date, the federal government did not owe money to anyone.

Texas was another important concern during President Jackson's second term. Jackson had always believed that Texas belonged to the United States, as part of the 1803 Louisiana Purchase. He blamed former President John Quincy Adams for signing away the rights to Texas in a treaty with Spain in 1819. After Mexico gained independence from Spain, the United States tried many times to purchase Texas but failed. Mexico allowed American settlers to cross the border and live in Texas. However, Americans who settled in Texas wanted the territory to become part of the United States.

In 1836, Texans, led by Jackson's old friend, Sam Houston, began a war for freedom from Mexico. One of the most famous battles of the war was fought at the Alamo, a fort near San Antonio that had once been a chapel. Here a group of almost two hundred Americans fought against an army of between five thousand and six thousand Mexican soldiers, led by the Mexican dictator, General Antonio Lopez de Santa Anna. For twelve days the Americans were heavily shelled. On the thirteenth day, March 6, 1836, the Mexicans captured the fort. All of the Americans were killed, including Davy Crockett, Colonel William B. Travis, and Jim Bowie. A convention had declared Texas independence four days earlier, but the Americans at the Alamo did not know this.

Sam Houston's army defeated Santa Anna's troops at the Battle of San Jacinto on April 21, 1836. Santa Anna was captured. He was forced to sign a treaty recognizing Texas independence, then released.

Many wanted President Jackson to name Texas a state, but he hesitated. Would it look to the rest of the

SOURCE DOCUMENT

To the Senate of the United States.

The joint resolutions of Congress unanimously expressing their sensibility on the intelligence of the death of General Lafayette, were communicated, in compliance with their will, to George Washington Lafayette, and the other members of the family of that illustrious man. By their request I now present the heartfelt acknowledgments of the surviving descendants of our beloved friend for that highly valued proof of the sympathy of the United States.

Andrew Jackson

Washington, 16th Dec. 1834.

This 1834 letter from President Jackson to the Senate expresses sympathy after the death of the Marquis de Lafayette, a French hero of the American Revolution.

world like he had started the war with Mexico just to take Texas? Would it reopen the slavery question and anger the North, again threatening the Union? On March 3, 1837, the day before Jackson's second and final term in office ended, Congress recognized Texas independence. This paved the way for Texas to become a state. Texas became a state in 1845.

Critics said Jackson mishandled relations with Mexico from the beginning. His first mistake may have been to send Anthony Butler as minister to Mexico. Butler was tactless and dishonest. He insulted the Mexican government by trying to bribe officials. President Jackson added to the insult by taking too long to recall Butler.

One event that took place during Jackson's second term in office showed how much the country was changing. While the people did not always agree with Presidents George Washington through John Quincy Adams, they seldom threatened the men in office. By the time Jackson was elected, however, the President was more available—and more often blamed for any unhappiness. Near the end of his second term, Jackson had received more than five hundred death threats. However, he said he was not worried about being murdered: "I try to live my life as if death might come at any moment."[10]

Presidents did not yet have bodyguards, so there was no one protecting Jackson on January 30, 1835, when a man tried to shoot him. Jackson had gone to the

Capitol Building for a funeral service held in the House Chambers. When he came out of the building, a well-dressed, bearded young man waited as the President walked toward him. He drew a small revolver from his pocket, aimed at Jackson's chest, and fired. The gun misfired and no bullet was discharged.

Before Jackson could recover, the man drew a second gun and fired again. Again the gun misfired. Jackson rushed at the man with his cane raised high over his head. He would have beaten him if bystanders had not thrown the would-be killer to the ground. The

This is a sketch of the attempted murder of President Jackson, drawn by an eyewitness. Both of Richard Lawrence's two pistols misfired, giving Jackson time to raise his cane against the would-be assassin.

shooter, an unemployed English housepainter named Richard Lawrence, was taken away by police. Jackson appeared shaken. Later, when Martin Van Buren visited him at the White House, Jackson was playing with the Donelson children. He seemed unconcerned that he had nearly been killed.

Lawrence raved that Jackson had killed his father, but his parents had never been in the United States. Lawrence also claimed to be the British royal heir and said Jackson had kept him from assuming the throne. He was tried on April 11, 1835, found not guilty by reason of insanity and committed to an insane asylum.

Many people, including Jackson himself, saw the President's escape from death as a sign of divine protection. As a result, fondness and respect for Jackson grew. By the time he left office on March 4, 1837, Old Hickory was the most popular President in the history of the United States.

7

THE JACKSONIAN AGE

President Andrew Jackson left office on the day his replacement, Martin Van Buren, was inaugurated. People had again traveled long distances to Washington, D.C., to see their hero. This time they had come to say good-bye to Jackson. The crowd cheered as he walked down the steps of the Capitol for the last time. "At Van Buren's inauguration, all eyes were on the outgoing President," Thomas Hart Benton wrote later. "For once, the rising was eclipsed by the setting sun."[1]

President Jackson had presided over an important period of time in American history. In fact, the fifty years between the War of 1812 and the Civil War is called the Jacksonian Age. That period of time has also been called the Jackson Revolution, because of the sweeping changes that took place in American society and politics.

The Industrial Revolution was responsible for many of the changes that took place in the United States during the Jacksonian Age. The "go ahead" American spirit and plenty of natural resources such as coal, water power, and immigrant labor, made the United States ripe for industrialization.[2]

The growth of industry in America was helped along by Samuel Slater, an English mechanic and textile worker. He copied English machine designs and opened a cotton mill in Providence, Rhode Island, in 1793. That same year, the supply of cotton was greatly increased by Eli Whitney's invention of the cotton gin (a machine for removing the seeds from cotton). The American textile

SOURCE DOCUMENT

... in order to maintain the Union unimpaired it is absolutely necessary that the laws passed by the constituted authorities should be faithfully executed in every part of the country, and that every good citizen should at all times stand ready to put down, with the combined force of the nation, every attempt at unlawful resistance.

(Farewell Address, March 4, 1837)

In his Farewell Address when leaving the presidency, Andrew Jackson expressed his desire that the Union of the United States be maintained at all costs.

industry prospered.[3] (In the early 1800s, Andrew Jackson was one of twenty-four farmers in his county who owned a cotton gin. He rented the gin to other growers for a fee.)[4]

Improved roads, railroads, and canals for transportation added to Jacksonian Age progress. The National Road, from Cumberland, Maryland, to Vandalia, Illinois, a distance of eight hundred miles, was begun in 1811 and completed in 1852. The Erie Canal, linking the Hudson River, near Albany, New York, to Lake Erie, at Buffalo, New York, was completed in 1825. Thus began an era of canal building that created more than forty-five hundred miles of canals in the United States.[5]

Many inventions during the Jacksonian Age improved the American way of life. Cyrus H. McCormick invented the mechanical reaper for harvesting grain in 1831, marking the beginning of the development of modern agriculture.[6] In 1836 Samuel Colt patented his revolver.[7] Charles Goodyear's process for vulcanizing rubber was developed in 1839.[8] Samuel F. B. Morse invented his first electromagnetic telegraph in 1836.[9]

During Jackson's time, almost two thirds of the workforce was still engaged in agriculture, but the American way of life was changing. As industrialization progressed, no longer did the entire family work together on its land to support the household. Men worked in factories or offices, and women stayed at home to keep the house and raise the children.

The standard of living increased for most workers. Still, as wages rose and some families did well, others were left out. Poverty grew. Smoke from factories polluted the air. Living conditions in cities were often overcrowded and unclean. For the first time, national and local governments passed measures, such as factory and sanitation laws, to improve social conditions.

The workers themselves also looked for ways to improve working and living conditions. They formed labor unions and political organizations. They supported those candidates for public office who promised to improve their lots in life.

As the American way of life changed, so, too, did the nation's political system. During the Jacksonian Age, political parties emerged as the federal government took responsibility for improving the lives of its citizens.

The Democratic party was formed in the 1820s as the result of a split in the Democratic-Republican party. Andrew Jackson was the first President elected from the Democratic party. (He ran as a Democratic-Republican, but by the time he was elected President in 1828, the name had been shortened to Democratic party.) Under Jackson's direction, the Democrats appealed most to farmers, laborers, and frontiersmen (women could not yet vote). The party was against the national bank, high taxes on imported goods, and spending federal money for national improvements, such as roads and canals.

The Whig party was formed about 1834 by members of the old National Republican party. Whigs opposed the policies of President Jackson. They wanted to reestablish the Second Bank of the United States. They also wanted the federal government to give the states the money received from the sale of public lands. The Whig party elected its first President, William Henry Harrison, in 1841. However, Harrison died of pneumonia on April 4, 1841, one month after his inauguration. Whig party leaders were Daniel Webster and Henry Clay. In 1844, Clay was his party's candidate for President, but he was defeated by Democrat James K. Polk. A Whig President was elected in 1848, when Zachary Taylor defeated Democratic candidate Lewis Cass. The Whig party began to fall apart in 1850, when members disagreed over slavery. Some members joined the Republican party and others became Democrats.

As President of the United States and leader of his party, Jackson played a major role in political change. His political beliefs have been labeled Jacksonian Democracy. Because he was widely admired, Old Hickory's candidacy for President encouraged more people to take part in the government. They voted for their hero, then followed more closely the activities of the government because he was in office.

Jackson's campaigns for President also introduced the use of political tactics to sway public opinion. Never before had political parties tried to get votes for their candidates by promising the voters a better life. Unfortunately, the campaigns of 1828 and 1832 also

This portrait of Old Hickory was painted in 1845, about eight years after he left the presidency.

used mudslinging as never before, as a way of putting down the other side's candidate.

Many political changes occurred during Jackson's presidency. National political conventions were held for the first time. Third parties, including the Anti-Masonic, Nullifier, and the Workingmen's parties, ran candidates for office.

Jackson is credited with expanding the power and status of the office of President. He was a strong leader, who believed the President should not simply follow Congress. Before Jackson, Presidents vetoed legislation only when they considered it unconstitutional. However, Jackson used the veto twelve times—more than it was used by any President before him. Jackson was the first President to use his power of the veto for political reasons, making it a legislative tool.

President Jackson also used his executive power in presenting bills to Congress that he wanted passed. This was in strong contrast to the four Whig Presidents who came after him. William Henry Harrison, John Tyler, Zachary Taylor, and Millard Fillmore stuck strictly to earlier interpretations of the Constitution and left legislative matters to Congress.

Both during his lifetime and after, Andrew Jackson caused controversy. Some thought of him as a mean-tempered, hot-headed President, who disregarded the Constitution. Others saw him as a hero, who saved the Union and renewed the spirit of democracy for Americans.

Sarah Yorke married Andrew Jackson's adopted son, Andrew Jackson, Jr., on November 24, 1831. She helped take care of her father-in-law in his later years.

Historians argue on both sides. Jackson's admirers say that his confidence in the Union gave Americans respect for the past and hope for the future. Others say he was a mean, poorly educated man who hurt the country more than he helped it.

Andrew Jackson, the people's hero, was ill and worn out when he left Washington in March 1837, after eight years in office. He had lost most of his teeth and looked older than his seventy years. Always too thin, he now seemed frail.

Nearly all of his adult life, Jackson had been in pain from old wounds. He also suffered severe internal bleeding from an abscess in his chest cavity. The abscess, or pocket of infection, was caused by the bullet Jackson carried near his heart. The bleeding episodes increased as he aged and each one left him weaker. Doctors used a common treatment for that time; they opened a vein and let it bleed. Jackson also treated himself with home remedies that may have done more harm than good. At various times he took calomel, which is a compound of mercury and salt. Today we know that too much salt can be harmful and mercury is actually poisonous to the human body. Jackson probably survived the medical treatments only because of his strong constitution and sheer force of will.

Although he had looked forward to going home to the Hermitage, Jackson's last few years were difficult. (His home had burned down in 1833, but since then had been completely rebuilt.) After his retirement,

A grumpy Andrew Jackson posed for this photograph without his false teeth sometime in 1845. (The early photographs were called daguerreotypes.)

Jackson had to rebuild his fortune. Andrew Jackson, Jr., had been left in charge at the Hermitage, but he was a poor business manager. After he left office, Jackson worked to repay nearly fifteen thousand dollars in debts incurred by Andrew, Jr.[10]

In the last eight years of his life, Andrew Jackson paid off all of his debts. He also continued to take part in politics, campaigning for Martin Van Buren and, later, endorsing James K. Polk for President.

Sarah Yorke, the wife of Andrew Jackson, Jr., helped to care for the ex-President after he retired to the Hermitage.

Jackson was seventy-eight years old when he died on June 8, 1845, eight years after leaving office. His family, friends, and loyal household servants were with him at the end. Old Hickory was buried in the Hermitage garden, next to his beloved Rachel.

Jackson had come to Washington a sick man, grief-stricken over the death of his wife. Yet, he became a strong, powerful President, who earned the loyalty of the Americans he served.

Robert V. Remini, who has written more about Andrew Jackson than any other historian, claims that his contributions to the nation were impressive and his faults were often overstated. Remini sums up the man and his presidency:

"In sum, then, I regard Jackson's unquenchable love of the Union and his unshakable trust in democracy as the most admirable things about him and his great legacy to future generations of Americans."[11]

Chronology

1767—Andrew Jackson is born in the Waxhaws, South Carolina.

1780—Fights against the British in the American
-1781   Revolution.

1781—Mother, Elizabeth Hutchinson Jackson, dies.

1784—Moves to Salisbury, North Carolina, and studies
-1786   law.

1787—Licensed as an attorney in North Carolina.

1788—Fights his first duel, with Waightstill Avery.

1791—Marries Rachel Donelson Robards for the first time.

1794—Remarries Rachel.

1796—Elected to serve in the United States House of Representatives.

1797—Elected to United States Senate.

1802—Elected major general of Tennessee militia.

1804—Purchases Hermitage property.

1805—Participates in Aaron Burr conspiracy.

1806—Kills Charles Dickinson in a duel.

1809—Adopts son of Elizabeth and Severn Donelson; the baby is named Andrew Jackson, Jr.

1812—Leads troops against Native Americans and
-1815   British; nicknamed "Old Hickory."

1813—Gunfight with the Bentons; adopts Lyncoya.

1814—Arrives in New Orleans.

1815—Halts British advance against New Orleans.

1818—Orders executions of Robert Ambrister and Alexander Arbuthnot for treason.

1822—Nominated for President by the Tennessee legislature.

1823—Elected United States senator.

1825—Defeated for President in House election.

1825—Nominated for President by the Tennessee legislature.

1828—Elected President of the United States; Rachel dies.

1830—Signs Indian Removal Bill.

1831—Accepts cabinet resignations and appoints new cabinet.

1832—Reelected President.

1833—Force Bill message sent to Congress; dismisses William Duane.

1834—Censured by Senate; the Hermitage burns.

1835—Escapes assassination attempt.

1836—Issues Specie Circular; rebuilding of the Hermitage completed.

1837—Issues Farewell Address; leaves White House for the Hermitage.

1838—Suffers severe hemorrhage (bleeding) attacks.

1840—Campaigns for Martin Van Buren.

1844—Endorses James K. Polk for President.

1845—Dies and is buried next to his wife, Rachel, at the Hermitage.

Chapter Notes

Chapter 1

1. William Gutman, *Andrew Jackson and the New Populism* (New York: Barron's Educational Series, Inc., 1987), p. 138.

2. Burke Davis, *Old Hickory: A Life Of Andrew Jackson* (New York: The Dial Press, 1977), p. 227.

3. Ibid., p. 226.

4. Ibid.

5. Marquis James, *Andrew Jackson: Portrait of a President* (New York: The Bobbs–Merrill Company, 1937), p. 165.

6. Davis, p. 230.

7. Robert V. Remini, *The Life of Andrew Jackson* (New York: Harper & Row Publishing, 1988), p. 176.

8. Ibid., p. 179.

9. Arthur M. Schlesinger, Jr., *The Age of Jackson* (Boston: Little, Brown and Company, 1946), p. 6.

10. Ibid.

11. Remini, p. 181.

Chapter 2

1. William Gutman, *Andrew Jackson and the New Populism* (New York: Barron's Educational Series, Inc., 1987), p. 18.

2. Burke Davis, *Old Hickory: A Life Of Andrew Jackson* (New York: The Dial Press, 1977), p. 5.

3. Ibid., p. 6.

4. Marquis James, *Andrew Jackson: The Border Captain* (New York: Grosset and Dunlap, 1933), p. 2.

5. Ibid., p. 28.

6. Ibid., p. 29.

Chapter 3

1. Robert V. Remini, *Andrew Jackson and the Course of American Empire 1767–1821* (New York: Harper & Row Publishing, 1977), p. 28.

2. Burke Davis, *Old Hickory: A Life Of Andrew Jackson* (New York: The Dial Press, 1977), p. 8.

3. Remini, *Andrew Jackson and the Course of American Empire 1767–1821*, p. 38.

4. Davis, p. 16.

5. Ibid., p. 17.

6. Ibid., p. 21.

7. Marquis James, *Andrew Jackson: Portrait of a President* (New York: The Bobbs-Merrill Company, 1937), p. 24.

8. Remini, *Andrew Jackson and the Course of American Empire 1767–1821*, p. 136.

9. Robert V. Remini, *The Revolutionary Age of Andrew Jackson* (New York: Harper & Row Publishing, 1976), p. 21.

Chapter 4

1. Arthur M. Schlesinger, Jr., *The Almanac of American History* (New York: Bramhall House, 1983), p. 192.

2. Robert V. Remini, *Andrew Jackson and the Course of American Empire 1767–1821* (New York: Harper & Row Publishing, 1977), p. 180.

3. Ibid., p. 181.

4. Ibid., p. 227.

5. Burke Davis, *Old Hickory: A Life Of Andrew Jackson* (New York: The Dial Press, 1977), p. 105.

6. Ibid., p. 107.

7. James C. Curtis, *Andrew Jackson and the Search for Vindication* (Boston: G. K. Hall & Co., 1976), p. 120.

8. "New Orleans, Battle of," *Microsoft Encarta 96 Encyclopedia, 1993–1995*, Microsoft Corporation, Funk & Wagnalls Corporation.

9. Davis, p. 149.

Chapter 5

1. Robert V. Remini, *Andrew Jackson and the Course of American Freedom 1822–1832* (New York: Harper & Row Publishing, 1981), p. 59.

2. Burke Davis, *Old Hickory: A Life Of Andrew Jackson* (New York: The Dial Press, 1977), p. 208.

3. Arthur M. Schlesinger, Jr., *The Almanac of American History* (New York: Bramhall House, 1983), p. 214.

4. Remini, pp. 95-96.

5. Schlesinger, p. 218.

6. *Congressional Quarterly, Cabinets and Counselors—The President and the Executive Branch* (Washington, D.C.: Congressional Quarterly, Inc., 1989), p. 59.

7. William Gutman, *Andrew Jackson and the New Populism* (New York: Barron's Educational Series, Inc., 1987), p. 147.

8. James C. Curtis, *Andrew Jackson and the Search for Vindication* (Boston: G. K. Hall & Co., 1976), p. 204.

9. Ibid., p. 203.

Chapter 6

1. *1995 Information Please Almanac* (New York: Houghton Mifflin Company, 1995), p. 639.

2. Robert V. Remini, *Andrew Jackson and the Course of American Freedom 1822–1832* (New York: Harper & Row Publishing, 1981), pp. 236–237.

3. William Gutman, *Andrew Jackson and the New Populism* (New York: Barron's Educational Series, Inc., 1987), p. 150.

4. Robert V. Remini, *Andrew Jackson and the Course of American Democracy 1833–1845* (New York: Harper & Row Publishing, 1984), p. 23.

5. Ibid., p. 25.

6. Gutman, p. 151.

7. Remini, *Andrew Jackson and the Course of American Democracy 1833–1845*, p. 102.

8. Burke Davis, *Old Hickory: A Life Of Andrew Jackson* (New York: The Dial Press, 1977), p. 335.

9. Ibid., p. 287.

10. Ibid., p. 345.

Chapter 7

1. William Gutman, *Andrew Jackson and the New Populism* (New York: Barron's Educational Series, Inc., 1987), p. 156.

2. Robert V. Remini, *The Revolutionary Age of Andrew Jackson* (New York: Harper & Row Publishing, 1976), p. 5.

3. *Webster's Guide to American History* (Springfield, Mass: G. & C. Merriam Company Publishers, 1971), pp. 1236–1237.

4. Robert V. Remini, *Andrew Jackson and the Course of American Empire 1767–1821* (New York: Harper & Row Publishing, 1977), p. 134.

5. "Canal," *Microsoft Encarta 96 Encyclopedia, 1993–1995* Microsoft Corporation, Funk & Wagnalls Corporation.

6. Ibid., "McCormick, Cyrus Hall".

7. Ibid., "Handgun".

8. Ibid., "Rubber".

9. Ibid., "Morse, Samuel Finley Breese".

10. Robert V. Remini, *Andrew Jackson and the Course of American Democracy 1833–1845* (New York: Harper & Row Publishing, 1984), p. 462.

11. Remini, *The Revolutionary Age of Andrew Jackson*, p. xvii.

Further Reading

Davis, Burke. *Old Hickory: A Life Of Andrew Jackson.* New York: The Dial Press, 1977.

Gutman, William. *Andrew Jackson and the New Populism.* New York: Barron's Educational Series, Inc., 1987.

James, Marquis. *Andrew Jackson: The Border Captain.* New York: Grosset and Dunlap, 1933.

Osinski, Alice. *Encyclopedia of Presidents: Andrew Jackson.* Chicago: Children's Press, 1987.

Remini, Robert V. *Andrew Jackson and the Course of American Democracy 1833–1845.* New York: Harper & Row Publishing, 1984.

———. *Andrew Jackson and the Course of American Empire 1767–1821.* New York: Harper & Row Publishing, 1977.

———. *Andrew Jackson and the Course of American Freedom 1822–1832.* New York: Harper & Row Publishing, 1981.

———. *The Life of Andrew Jackson.* New York: Harper & Row Publishing, 1988.

———. *The Revolutionary Age of Andrew Jackson.* (New York: Harper & Row Publishing, 1976.

Internet Sites

University of South Florida Tampa Campus Library, President Andrew Jackson

> http://www.lib.usf.edu/spccoll/guide/p/pres/
> jackson.html

Encyclopedia Americana: Andrew Jackson

> http://www.grolier.com/presidents/ea/bios/
> 07pjack.html

Andrew Jackson—Graphics version, Fun Facts

> http:/www.whitehouse.gov/WH/glimpse/presidents/
> html/aj7-plain.html

Andrew Jackson's Hermitage—Virtual Educational Tour

> http://gaia.earthwatch.org/x/Xmckee.html

Index

JA 08 04

J921
JACK
1-5-04
21.00